inland AUSTRALIA

Little Hills Press

Manning the gates of a stockyard in northern Queensland. The cattle industry in Australia is one of the country's important export earners.

The Road around Uluru (Ayers Rock) the world's largest monolith. Situated in Central Australia it is of spiritual significance to the Anangu people.

Mount Conner, 'the forgotten residual of Central Australia' is a sprawling sandstone mesa about 90 kilometres east of Uluru (Ayers Rock). Part of the Curtin Springs property it can be climbed on the south side. It changes colours from soft pinks to dusty reds depending on time of day and year.

Burning off - a common sight in certain canefields prior to harvesting.

*Sunset from the
Mt Lofty Ranges
in South Australia.*

An aboriginal rock painting found in the Northern Territory. Perhaps the best known is Obiri Roack in Kakadu National Park. The paintings are not an idea of the moment but rather a honed down record of essential aspects of their culture.

Alexandra Cave, Naracoorte Caves Conservation Park, South Australia. The stalactites are deposits of calcium carbonate in the form of icicles hanging from the roof of the cave and are formed by dripping water. The deposits standing on the floor are called stalagmites.

Kangaroos are synonymous with Australia. No matter what the species, they are a herbivorous marsupial mammal with developed legs that are used for jumping.

Northern Australia is Crocodile Country, and this `saltie' can grow to 6.4 metres (21 feet) in length.

Kimberley waterhole, a lush oasis in northern Australia, shows the effects of water in an arid climate.

*Katherine Gorge,
Northern Territory.*

Mt Field National Park, Tasmania.

These beautiful rainforest areas are some 30 degree latitude apart. A testament to the amazing variability of climate on the island continent.

Cedar Creek Falls, Queensland.

Sugar Cane Farming near Mackay. The district produced about one third of Australia's total sugar crop. Certain strains of sugar are still torched between June and December before harvesting.

An old abandoned homestead very much part of the landscape in rural Australia.

Uluru (Ayers Rock), the monolith in the middle of the vast continent, is a mecca for tourists worldwide.

Victoria River in Gregory National Park in the Northern Territory.

Typical Australian foliage - the gum tree windblown and scraggy but still there.

Worked land in south east Australia used mainly for grazing cattle and running sheep.

Vineyards in the Barossa Valley, South Australia.

The old Post and Telegraph Station at Willunga township, South Australia.

The solitude of the Australian wilderness at dusk.

Sheep enjoy the early morning sun on a winter's day. Australia presently pastures about 64 million sheep.

*Country town cricket
during the summer.
(Wingen, New South Wales)*

The Derwent River near New Norfolk, Tasmania.

Sunset in Outback Australia.

A frosty winter's morning in the New South Wales countryside just north of the nation's capital, Canberra.

Thredbo Creek, Snowy Mountains in winter.

A church silhouetted against the sky in the Snowy Mountains.

Mount Roland. Though the mountains in Australia are not high (Australia's highest mountain, Mt Kosciusko is 2,230 metres [7314 feet] high) they dominate the landscape. The sandstone formations especially have proved difficult to traverse.

Frozen gum (eucalypt) leaves in winter.

Little Hills and Murrurundi as seen from the Pass on the crown of the Liverpool Range.

Little Hills Press Pty Ltd
Sydney, Australia
ISBN 186315 140 0
email: info@littlehills.com
http:\\www.littlehills.com
(c) Photographs, Little Hills Press, November 1999. Concept Chris Baker
Design and development Artitude.
Editorial Team: Sam Lynch, Mark Truman.
Cover - Overlooking the National Park, Mt Field, Tasmania. Photography credits - pages:
Eduard Domin, 1, 2, 4, 5, 7, 11, 12, 13, 14, 15, 19, 20, 21, 22, 23, 25, 27, 28, 29, 30, 31.
Gonzalo de Alvear 3, 8, 16, 18.
Katherine Tourist Office 10, 11, 17, 26.
Chris Baker 24, 32.
Outback Queensland Tourism Authority 8, 26. Northern Territory Tourism Commission 6, 9.
Printed in Singapore